GW01340025

A Pound of Fine Flower

A Pound of Fine Flower

RECIPES FROM A LINCOLNSHIRE VILLAGE BAKERY OF THE 1830S

Teresa Crompton

☙

Castle Yard Books

Published by:
Castle Yard Books
The Barn
Castle Farm
Castle Bytham
Grantham
Lincolnshire
NG33 4RJ

© Teresa Crompton 1997

With thanks to Joan Greetham

The line illustrations are reproduced by kind permission of the Rural History Centre, University of Reading.

The right of Teresa Crompton to be identified as the author of *A Pound of Fine Flower* has been asserted generally in accordance with sections 77 and 78 of the Copyright, Design and Patents Act 1988.

ISBN: 0 9529122 0 1

All rights reserved. No part of this publication may be reproduced, stored in a retrieval system or transmitted in any form by any means, electronic, mechanical, photocopying, recording or otherwise except brief extracts for the purpose of review without the written permission of the publisher.

Printed and bound by Advanced Laser Press Ltd., Longstanton, Cambridge, England.

Contents

Preface   1

The Story of the Old Cookery Book   6

'Falkingham and Neighbourhood'   9

Note   13

The Recipes   15

Cakes and Biscuits   17

Puddings   29

Preserves   31

Beverages   35

Miscellaneous   39

Glossary   43

Index   48

To Preserve Grapes Whole

Take some close Bunches
of either white or red common
ripe not too ripe and
lay them in a Jar put to
them a quarter of a pound
of sugar candy and fill
the Jar with common
Brandy tie them down
close with a bladder and
set them in a dry place

Damson Wine

After you have gather'd your
damsons put them on a
dry day weigh them and
then Bruise them put
them into a Jar then
as cook up its add to
every pound of fruit just
a gallon of water Boil the
water skim it and pour it
scalding hot on your fruit
when it's had three or four days
drawing of it then put it into
a vessel and to every gallon of
Liquid put 2 and fifty of sugar
fill up the vessel and as it takes
to close and the longer it
stands the better when
you draw it off put a lump
of sugar into every bottle

Ginger Wine

Put 2 lb of Lisbon Sugar with
4 gallons of spring Water Boil
them a quarter of an hour
and keep skimming it add
the same when the Liquor
is cold squeeze in the
Juice of 2 Lemons then
Boil the Peel the

Preface

England in the 1830s

'Old opinions, feelings - ancestral customs and institutions - are crumbling away,' wrote the novelist Bulwer Lytton in 1833, 'and both the spiritual and temporal worlds are darkened by the shadow of change.'

By the mid 1830s, the population of Great Britain was fifteen million. Although more than half still lived in rural areas, the shift from the countryside to towns and cities was well under way.

The country was rapidly becoming smaller. Since the beginning of the industrial revolution, the road and rail networks had undergone enormous expansion. Whereas in 1750 the journey by coach from London to Edinburgh, for example, had taken ten days, by 1830 the time had fallen to forty-six hours. Travel had formerly been an uncomfortable and dangerous privilege of the wealthy. Now, travel for its own sake was available to the burgeoning middle classes. And, with the freer flow of people and goods, came the rapid spread of ideas.

The 1830s witnessed other social and economic changes. In 1833 slavery was abolished in the British Empire. In 1835, the year Halley's Comet re-appeared, the first negative photograph was taken by William Henry Fox Talbot. A disastrous fire gutted the Houses of Parliament and the competition for the design of a new building (the present one) was won by a gothic, rather than a classical style. The new had triumphed over the old.

William IV, the 'Sailor King,' was on the throne. Already sixty-four years old when his reign began in 1830, he had married hastily in order to produce a legitimate heir. Two little girls were the result of this union but neither survived infancy. William himself was to die in 1838, and the crown pass to his young niece, Victoria.

The Duke of Wellington, so famous that cakes, as well as boots, were named after him, was in his sixties. In London, Dickens, only in his early twenties, was already scribbling furiously (*The Pickwick Papers* was produced in 1837). Florence Nightingale was still a girl in her teens and, up in Yorkshire, Charlotte Bronte was busy teaching her sisters, Emily and Ann, at Haworth Parsonage. Meanwhile, in the rectory at Somersby, Lincolnshire, the young Alfred Tennyson, in his twenties, was bemoaning the lukewarm reception of his first published book of poetry.

Local Life

But life in Folkingham carried on more or less as it had done for centuries. The 1834 entry from Pigot and Co.'s Lincolnshire Directory (reproduced on page 9) yields much information as to the everyday lives of the inhabitants.

An unusual feature of the village was the House of Correction with its impressive stone front. At the time of the 1841 census it housed 35 'prisoners.' In addition, a Governor, Matron, and two 'Turnkeys' lived on the premises. Most of the inmates were local, all but six having been born in the county. They were aged between fourteen and fifty but only eleven were women. Under the census heading 'occupation,' four are listed as 'tramp.' The other prisoners were labourers, servants, a groom, a drover, a shoemaker, a sawyer, a carrier, a bricklayer, and a tobacco manufacturer.

The George Family
It was in Folkingham that the George family, the writers of the recipes in this book, carried on their livelihood - providing the villagers with daily bread and baked goods.

William George kept the baker's shop in the Market Place and, over the years 1833 to 1838, he and his children jotted down an occasional 'receipt' in a small notebook, until there were fifty-seven in all. The notebook, now tatty and faded, is the source of the recipes in A *Pound of Fine Flower* and is in the possession of Mr Alan Crawford of Castle Bytham, Lincolnshire.

The origin of the recipes is unknown; perhaps they were passed on by friends, culled from books of the day, or dreamed up for trial in the bakery.

William George, the infant son of Robert George, baker, and his wife Mary, was baptised in St. Andrew's church, Folkingham, on December 2nd, 1786. Thirty years later, in the same church, William married Catharine Berridge, born in the parish of St. Martin's, Stamford, and over the following thirteen years the couple produced ten children, of whom perhaps eight survived infancy.

The children grew up in Market Place, in a tall, three storeyed house with two dormer windows set into its thick thatch. Downstairs a large window displayed the baked goods to passersby. The house still stands, although now reduced in height, without its thatch, and much altered. It is number 33. Next door, where numbers 29 and 31 stand today, was the Green Man Inn, demolished in 1869.

The Georges' bakehouse was down the jitty to the side of the house. The building has now been converted to a dwelling but it formerly contained two old brick built ovens.

Between 1833 and 1838, the years covered by the cookery book, those of the George children whose signatures appear in the cookery book were in their teens. They are Mary (born 1819), William (born 1821), Elizabeth (born 1822), Ann (born 1824), and Robert (born 1825). Robert George senior died during the period of the book's compilation, on July 15th, 1836, aged 78.

It was Robert junior who took over the family business. Robert married Matilda, born at Gedney Dyke, who was ten years younger than he. Matilda died in 1902 but Robert lived on for another six years. They are buried in Folkingham churchyard.

According to the 1871 and 1881 census returns, Robert and Matilda had seven children; Sarah, Christopher, Catherine, Florence, Francis William, John, and Minnie. Francis William (always known as 'Billy') was to be the last of the Georges to keep the family business. He carried on until about 1915 when, perhaps discouraged by the death of his wife, Mary Jane, in 1913, he left the village. The couple had no children.

When Billy departed from Folkingham the bakery trade was left to a business further down the hill - the shop being in the premises now known as 'Quaintways' whilst the buildings across the yard, now converted, formed the bakehouse.

For the information about the bakeries I am indebted to Mr John H M Andrews, formerly of Chapel Lane. He moved to the village from Bingham in 1933 and was employed at the Quaintways bakery by the Wollatons. He remembers meeting Billy George, by then living in Peterborough, who still owned and let out at least four houses in Folkingham.

Bread Pudding

1 Penny Loaf Grated fine
Put to it half pint of New
milk and a little Cream
if you have it with Whites
are fine Sugar a little
Brandy and a few Currans
if you like them Baked
put them in Cups

A Baked Custard Pudding

Mix 3 yolks of Eggs well beaten
with a spoonefull of flour
into a pint of new milk ad
some Sugar and Nutmeg
pour this into a dish and
cover the top with slices
of Bread ½ an hour will
Nicely Bake it

The Story of the Old Cookery Book

❦

The tale of how my family came into possession of the Georges' cookery book is an interesting one. I will let my father, Mr Alan Crawford of Castle Bytham, Lincolnshire, tell it in his own words:

"My father was born in 1884, the youngest of six children and the only boy. He grew up at South Lodge Farm, Pickworth, and from the age of five to eleven, walked the two-and-a-half miles to Folkingham every morning to go to school.

The school was down the hill below a bakery and afterwards Father would go into the shop and buy a halfpenny or penny bun to eat on his long walk home. The baker, Mr George, had a son called Billy. Although Billy was fifteen years older than Father, the two got on well together. As Billy and Father's family were Wesleyans, it could be that they met at the Chapel, too.

Then my grandfather retired and Father took the tenancy of the Home Farm at Culverthorpe. Time passed, life moved on. Father married, then joined the army, and he lost touch with the George family.

When he came out of the army in 1919 Father made several more moves in the space of ten years. Firstly, he went down to Hampshire, where I was born in 1923. Soon we came to Oxney Farm near Peterborough.

Shortly after our arrival there a baker came round in his van to see if he could supply us with bread on a regular basis. Father, who was having his meal in the kitchen while Mother chatted at the door, heard a voice he was sure he recognised. Getting up, he went to see who it was – and there stood Billy George!

Father and Billy rejoiced at seeing each other again after so many years. Billy, it turned out, had sold up his business at Folkingham and come to work in Peterborough for Fowlers, a big baking firm. It became a regular thing then for us to go to see Billy and his wife at their house in Dogsthorpe Road, when we went into Peterborough.

Billy was a little short chap, round and jolly, and when he laughed he rocked backwards and forwards in his armchair. He was very fond of talking about his 'twissies', I remember:

'I don't like this modern bread,' he'd say. 'I always liked those twissies we used to make at Folkingham. You hold them in the middle and give them a twist at this end, and a twist at that end...'

After we moved to Castle Bytham, twenty-five miles from Peterborough, in 1928, the Georges came out to see us occasionally. And we still visited them a couple of times a year; in the summer we'd have tea on their lawn, and a few days before Christmas, when we went to Peterborough market to sell our fatted geese, we'd go up to Dogsthorpe Road afterwards. Billy always had on his shiny suit in honour of our visit, and Mrs George laid on a big spread.

Sarah George was a nice, kindly woman. She was Billy's second wife (his first, Mary Jane, having died in

1913), and had already been a widow when they married. Neither she nor Billy had any children. The interesting thing was that Mrs George had previously lived at Castle Bytham with her first husband, Browning Francis, and so she had known people here and told us tales of the village years ago.

In 1941 Billy took ill and died, aged 72; he is buried in Folkingham churchyard with his first wife. Then Mrs George brought Father various of Billy's belongings, including a heavy silver serviette ring engraved with his initials: 'FWG' – for 'Francis William George' – and the old family cookery books from the Folkingham bakery days.

'I'd like you to have these,' she said.

She continued to come and visit us in the summer, and at Christmas, when she stayed for a few days. Whenever she came to the village one of her chief concerns was her own burial – about which she talked at length. Her first husband had been buried in Castle Bytham cemetery. At the time of his burial Mrs George had paid for the grave to be brick lined so that, when the time came, her coffin could be placed on top of his.

But somehow it had come to Mrs George's ears that the brick-lining work had not been carried out and this was a great source of worry to her:

'I've been done down,' she'd say sorrowfully, 'and what am I going to do about it?' There didn't seem to be any answer to that one!

When the old lady died in 1955, aged eighty-nine, a branch of the George family died out with her. She is buried in Castle Bytham cemetery with her first husband."

The Barn	Alan Crawford
Castle Farm	1996
Castle Bytham	

FALKINGHAM AND NEIGHBOURHOOD.

Falkingham, or *Folkingham*, is a small market town, in the parish of its name, hundred of Aveland, in the parts of Kesteven, 106 miles from London, 27 S. by E. from Lincoln and 14 N.W. from Spalding; situate on the side of a hill, abounding in springs, in a healthy and fine sporting country, and on the main road between Lincoln and Peterborough. In the *one hundred and thirty one* manors in the country of Lincoln, Falkingham was included, and formed part of the immense possessions belonging to Gilbert de Gaund, who accompanied King William from Normandy. It was afterwards granted to Henry de Belamonte, or Beaumont (in the reign of Edward 1.) who, it was supposed, erected the castle, which, on account of its being defended for Charles I. was destroyed by Cromwell. To the south-east of the town is a large encampment, with a foss and vallum; within the area (in a square form) is a keep of raised earth, defended by a foss, capable of being filled with water from an adjoining brook, and at the north-east corner, on the outside, is a small fortified enclosure, no doubt intended to secure the water for the use of the garrison. In the year 1808 a new prison or house of correction was erected on the site of the ancient castle, at an expense of £6,600, which was defrayed by a rate on the county; and in 1825 a further sum of £8,000. was expended in making considerable additions. Within the walls are a chapel and a tread mill. The jurisdiction and superintendance of the prison are vested in the magistrates for the parts of Kesteven. The town consists chiefly of a large quadrangle: on the north side is the Greyhound Inn, which commands an extensive and picturesque view.

The church is a well-built structure, in the pointed style, having at the west end a handsome lofty tower, crowned with eight elegant light croketted pinnacles: it is dedicated to St. Andrew, and the living is a rectory with the vicarage of Laughton united, in the partronage of Sir Gilbert Heathcote, Bart. The free grammar school, here, is open to all the children of the parish; it is chiefly supported from the proceeds of lands, near the town, bequeathed by J. R. Brokesby, Esq., and other benefactions have been made to provide clothing for a certain number of the scholars. At a small village called Walcot, about a mile to the north-west of the town, is a chalybeate spring, renowned for its medicinal virtues; about two miles to the north-east was a Gilbertine priory, founded by Godwinus, a rich citizen of London, in the time of King John. Falkingham enjoys but very little trade; and the market, which is held on Thursday, is of but trifling importance. The fairs are, Ash-Wednesday and Palm-Monday, May 12th, November 10th and 22nd, for horses, sheep and tradesmen's goods. Stow green fair is held but one mile east of the town, and lasts from the 16th to the 19th June, for horses, and on the 3rd and 4th July, for hardware and agricultural implements: this is much resorted to both for business and pleasure. The parish (which has no dependent township) contained, by the parliamentary census for 1821, 759 inhabitants; and by that for 1831, 744 only.

POST OFFICE, Thomas Wing, *Post Master*.-Letters from London and the South arrive every morning at seven, and are despatched every evening at seven.-Letters from the North arrive every evening at seven, and are despatched every morning at seven.

GENTRY AND CLERGY.
Bailey Mr. John
Cookson Mrs.
Ellershaw Mrs. Ann
Morris Mr. Edward
Richardson Mrs. Mary
Ward Mr. William
Wilson Rev. John

PROFESSIONAL PERSONS.
Blomfield Charles, surgeon
Cropley Samuel, academy
Hall Miss., ladies' boarding academy
Headley William C. surgeon

Welbourne C. E. master of the grammar school

BANKERS.
Holt and Kewney (branch), Smith Hall, agent-(draw on Barclay, Bevan & Co. London)

INNS AND PUBLIC HOUSES.
Crown, Hannah Sharp
Five Bells, William Banks
Green Man, Thomas Mitchell
Greyhound Inn (posting and

commercial) Susannah Baily
Red Lion, John Harmston

SHOPKEEPERS & TRADERS.
Banks William, auctioneer
Bland Mary, ironmonger
Bland William, blacksmith
Briston John, boot & shoemaker
Brittain Edward, butcher
Burrus Robert, cooper
Carter Joseph, retailer of beer
Carter Thomas, baker & flour dealer
Casswell John, grocer, tallow chandler, and draper
Clifton Thomas, bookseller and hairdresser
Cocking Joseph, grocer & draper
Daniell William, printer - Thomas Clifton, agent
Diver Charles, tailor
Drewry Martha, shopkeeper
Eastland John, tanner
George Wm, baker & flour dealer
Gibbins James, boot & shoemaker
Gibson William, gardener
Hall Thomas, butcher
Harmston John, wheelwright
Harmston William, joiner
Hill John, butcher
Johnson Robert, tailor
Love Charles, tailor
Pickworth Ann, milliner
Redshaw James, saddler
Reynolds Michael, tailor
Sumners & Son, grocers and drapers
Sumners Henry, maltster
Tatham B. & W., stone masons
Torrington Edward, grocer & draper
Ward James, chymist & druggist
Wyer Daniel, farrier

COACHES

To LONDON, the *Royal Mail* (from Hull) calls at the Greyhound Inn, every evening at a quarter before seven- and the *Express*, every night (Sunday excepted) at eleven.
To HULL and LINCOLN, the *Royal Mail* (from London) every morning at a quarter before seven, and the *Express*, every morning at a quarter before six (Sunday excepted), both call at the Greyhound.

CARRIERS

To LONDON, Ashby's *Van* calls at Saml. Cropley's, every Tuesday, Thursday and Saturday.
To BILLINGBORO', a *Mail Gig*, daily.
To BOURNE, - Wilds, from the Five Bells, every Monday.
To GRANTHAM,- Howard, every Wednesday and Saturday.
To LINCOLN, Ashby's *Van*, every Monday, Wednesday and Friday.
To SLEAFORD,- Howard, every Monday.

From Pigot & Co.'s 1834 *Directory of Lincolnshire*, by J. Pigot & Co. 17 Basing-Lane, London, & 18, Fountain-Street, Manchester.

Note

ଓଷ

In order to give an authentic impression of the original notebook, the recipes are recorded here just as the George family wrote them down more than one-hundred-and-sixty years ago; spelling mistakes have been left in, punctuation is uncorrected. The recipes, however, were not categorised; I have ordered them for ease of reference.

Please note that the recipes have not been tried or tested, and success cannot be guaranteed. Many have no stated 'method' and none give a precise oven temperature. Some are intended for bulk production. In addition, ingredients have changed; the eggs we have today, for example, are twice the size of those used in the George bakery. Other foodstuffs, such as 'Naples biscuits,' are no longer available, and modern raising agents may not act in the same way as 'purlash' and 'villatic salts.'

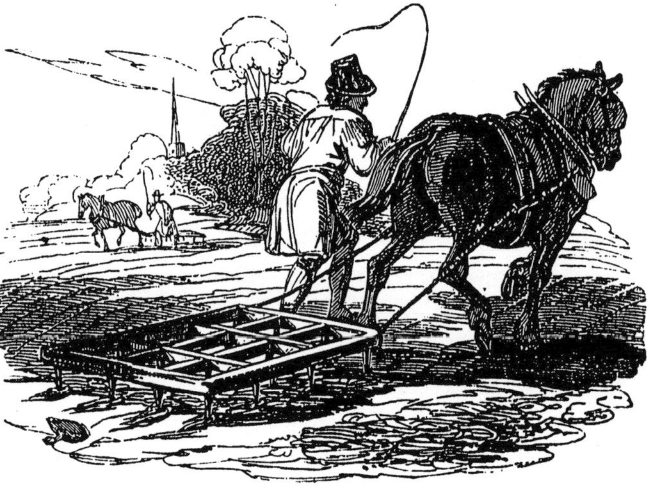

The Recipes

☙

How to make the Best Snap Gingerbread
Quarter of a stone of
Flour Quarter of a
stone Sixpenny Suger
Quarter of a Stone of Treac
le half a pound butter
1 Ounce of Ground Gin
ger Penneth of Essens
of Leamon Role the
Suger of a Board

How to make Queen Cakes
2 lb of fine Flour
1 lb of Butter
1 lb of Currants
1 lb of Lump Sugar
A little Bolleta Salt
6 Eggs
2 Ounces of Ground Rice
A little Leamon

Cakes and Biscuits

ઝ

How to make Shape Cakes

¼ stone of Fine Flower
½lb of Lump Sugar
½lb of Butter
Rub the Sugar and Butter togather in the Flower
2 small teaspoonfull of Villeta Salts.
Mix them togather with Old milk Rowl them out and cut them, with different sorts of Shapes

Almon Cakes

Mix ½lb of Flour
½lb Sifted Sugar
2 Ounces of Butter
2 Eggs leave out the white of one
1 Ounce of Bitter Almons
Beat Fine drop them on tins Bake them lightly

How to make The Best Snap Gingerbread

Quarter of a stone of Flour
Quarter of Stone Sixpenny Suger
Quarter of a Stone of Treacle
half a pound butter
1 Ounce of Ground Ginger
Penneth of Essens of Leamon
Role the Suger of a Board
    W George Folkingham

How to make The Best Gingerbread

Stone Flower,
4lbs of Treacle
3lbs of Sugar
3 Onces of Ginger
1 Once of Carrowe Seeds
1 Once of Curriander Seeds
2lbs of Butter
    Mary George

Abernethy Biscuits

2oz of butter rubbed in 2lb of flour
2oz Sugar soaked in
Mix it with milk and Water

Ginger Cakes (1)

Put into half a pound of Flower well dryed
two ounces of Butter
4 Ounces of loaf Sugar.
one Ounce of Ground Ginger
One Egg
a Spoonful of creem
make them into a past role very thin cut them into what
Shape you please and bake them

How to make Ginger Cakes (2)

To 2 lbs of Fine Flower
1lbs of Lump Sugar
6 Eggs
1 Ounce of the Best Ground Ginger
½ lb of Butter
Beat all well togagher
           1835 June 25th

Shrewsbury Cakes

½lb of Butter Rubbed in One Pound of Flower,
9 oz of L Sugar
2 Eggs
A few Carrow Seeds

How to make Tea Cakes

2lbs of Fine Flower
1lb of Currants
1lb of Butter
5 Eggs
A little Leamon
1lb of Lump Sugar

How to make Drop Cakes

1lb Butter Creame
1oz Sugar
4 Eggs
1½lb Flour
½oz Currants
Tolerable heat

Wellington Cakes

½lb of Butter rubbed in 1lb of Flower
10 Oz of Suggur
¼ Volatile Salts
3 Eggs
baked sole (slow ?) heat, it will make 36. at 1.. Each

Thick Gingerbread from Brigg

3lbs of Treacle
1½lb Moist Sugar
½lb of Butter
3lb of Flour
2 Eggs
Carrowseeds
a little yeast

Plain and Very Crispt Biscuits

Make a pound of Flour the yolk of an Egg and some milk into a very stiff past beat it well a knead till quite smooth roll very thin and cut into biscuits bake them in a slow oven till quite dry and Crisp 1834

Common Gingerbread (1)

½ Stone Flour
½ Stone Treacle
1lb of sugar
½ ounce ground Ginger
Penneth of Essens of Leamon
quarter of Butter
role the sugar well and mix in the treacle with your hand make it the night before you Bake it Give the snap Gingerbread a deal of room

How to make Common Gingerbread (2)

¾ Stone of Bread Flower
5lbs of Treacle
1lb of Butter
2 Onces and a half of purlash
Mealt the Butter and purlash togather With 1 Pint of Warter
3 Ounces of Ginger
1 Ounce of Carroway Seeds

How to make a Spunge Cake (1)

8 Onces of Fine Flower
½lb of Lump Sugur
6 Eggs Beat the wites and yoaks togather
A few drops of Leamon
Butter your shape well

How to make a Spunge Cake (2)

to ½lb of Fine Flower.
1lb of Lump Sugar to 12 Eggs Leave out 6 of the Wites
1 Table Spoonfull of Water
A few drops of Leamon
beat all well together

How to make Common Tea Cakes

3lbs of Fine Flower
1lb of Butter
1lb of Lump Suggur
8 Eggs
A few Carrow Seeds
A little Leamon
Rowl the paste thin and cut it out with a shape

Spice Cakes

Half a Pound of Butter beaten to a Cream
½ a lb of Suggar
1 Pound of Flower
6 Eggs
the Wites of three Eggs
one Nutmegg graited
beat all well together drop them on tins and bake them

How to make Finger Biscuits

1lb Lump Sugar.
4 Eggs.
1lb and 2 Onces of Fine Flower.
A little Leamon.
Long and very narrow.
            Oct 9th (1833)

How to make Plumb Cakes

4lb½ of Fine Flower
2lbs of Fine Powder Sugar
2lbs of Currants
1lbs of Butter
A small Cup of New Yeast,
It will make 4 1.6d Cakes and 1, 1.2d Ca
         Sept. 25, 1833

Rice Cakes (1)

½lb Butter Cream
½lb Sugar
1lb flour
¼lb Rice ground
7 eggs the sise of a nut

Rice Cakes (2)

Half a pound of Butter beaten to a Cream,
5 eggs. the yolks and wites bete Seperate
half Pound of Rice
3 Spoonfulls of Flower
half a lb of Sugur
a little Leamon Peal grated
the whole to be well beaten for twenty minits cups or molds
to be full and Half baked in a modarate Oven

Rice Cakes (3)

½lb Butter
½oz Sugar
½oz Flour
2oz Ground Rice
4 Eggs
Volatile Salts About the size of a nut

Rice Cakes (4)

Beet the yolk of fifteen Eggs for half an hour with a wisk then put to them 10 ounces of Loaf Sugar sifted fine mix them well together put in to the Ground Rice a little Orange, water of Brandy and the Rhines grate them put in the whites of 7 Eggs well beaten and stir the whole together for a quarter of an hour put them in a hoop and set it in a quick Oven for ½ an hour and they will be done

Maderia Buns

Take
6oz Butter
6oz Sugar
1oz Flour & 4 Eggs
The rind of one Leamon grated & the Juice
also villatic salts the same as the rice Cakes

How to make Queen Cakes (1)

½lb of Fine Flower
1lb of Butter
1lb of Currants
1lb of Lump Sugar
A little Velleta Salts
6 Eggs
2 Ounces of Ground Rice
A Little Leamon

How to make Queen Cakes (2)

lb½ of Fine Flower
½lb of Butter
1lb of Sugar
½lb of Currants
5 eggs
2 Onces of Ground rice
A little Leamon

How to make Pound Cake

1lb and 2 Onces of Fine Flower
2lbs of Currants well Dried
1lbs of Lump Sugar
One lb of Butter
9 Eggs beat the wites and yoaks togather
A few drops of Leamon or Brandy
Some Leamon Peal
Beat them all togather for 1 hour

Puddings

Bread Pudding

A Penny Loaf Grated fine
Put to it half pint of New milk and a little Cream if you have it with Whites and fine Sugar a little Brandy and a few Currants If you like them Baked put them in Cups

A Baked Custard Pudding

Mix 3 yolks of Eggs well beaten with a spoonful of flour into a pint of new milk add some Sugar and Nutmeg pour this into a dish and cover the top with Slices of Bread ½ an hour will Nicely Bake it.

Sago Pudding

Boil 2 Ounces of Sago into a pint of Milk til tender when could add 5 Eggs 2 Naples Biscuits a little Brandy and Sugar to your taste Boil it in a Basin and serve it up with Melted Butter and a little wine and sugar

Orange Budding

Bruise a quarter of a Pound of Candid Orange Peal in a morter then add 2 quarters of a lb of Naple Biscuits ¾ of a pound of sugar the yolk of 10 Eggs and one White Beaten together line the dish with paste Bake it 1 Hour add the Juice of 1 Leamon

Preserves

☙

To Bottle Green Currants

Gather your Currants when the sun is hot upon them then strip them from the stalks and Put them into Bottles Corke them Close set them in dry sand They will keep all Winter

To Preserve Grapes Whole

Takake some close Bunches weather white or red immaterial not two ripe and lay them in a Jar Put to them a quarter of a pound of sugar candy and fill the jar with common Brandy tie them down close with a bladder and set them in a dry place

Gooseberry Cheese

A peck of Red Goosberrys Boil or Baked in a Jar untill they will pulp through A sive then add 3 Pounds of powder Sugar and Boil it 3 hours then Fill Your Shapes

To Pickle Girkin

Chuse nice young Girkin lay them in Salt and Water for a few days then drain them on a sive when quite dry put them on a Jar and Cover them with Vine leaves Boil Vinegar and put Over them Repeating Vine leaves over morning and Boiling keep them moderatly warm when of a good Green tie them close down you may yse spice if you please Penneth Coin (?)

Apple Cheese

Take some Apples But do not pare them Boil them quite down squeese them through a sive put in sugar to your taste then Boil them again over a slow fire untill they leve the Pan and then put them into any shape you Please they will keep a year

To Clarify Sugar for Preserving

Put ½lb of Sugar into a pan with water enough to melt it then put in 12 Eggs whites free from the treadle and Beet it to a froth cover the Boiling sugar with this froth and Boil them to gather till the Sugar is clear remove the escum

Apple Cheese

Take some Apples But do not pare them quite down you set them through a sieve put in sugar to your taste then Boil them again over a slow fire untill they look the skin and then put them into any shape you please they will keep a year

Goosebery Cheese

Mash off the Goosebery's Boil & Bake in a Jar untill they will pulp through A sieve then add 3/4 pound of powder Sugar and Boil it 3 hours then fill your Shapes

How to make Anberry Vinegar

Take any quantity of rasps put white wine Vinegar upon them till they are covered an inch deep say about 1 Ib to 1/2 Pint let them stand a week or ten days, stir them frequently then to a Pint of juice add 1 Pound of Loaf Sugar

To Clarify Sugar for Preserving

Put 3 Ib of Sugar into a pan with water enough to melt it then put in 1 Egg white free from the treacle and Beet it to a froth over the Boiling Suger with this froth and them to gather till the Sugar is clear remove the scum

Beverages

⊗

How to make Rasberry Vinager

Take any quantity of rasps put white wine Vinegar upon them till they are covered an inch deep say about 1lb to ½ Pint let them stand a week strain them frequently skim it to a pint of Juice and 1 Pound of Loaf Sugar

How to make Slow Wine

To half a peck of slows to 1 gallond of water put your water boiling hot over the slows and let it stand three or four days Drain the licquer from the slows add to it 3 pounds and a ½ of good powder sugar
    1835 Oct 9th

How to make Ginger Wine (1)

To 4 Gallons of Water
1 Stone of the beast Powder Sugar.
6 Ounces of the Best Base Ginger
8 Leamons.
6 Oranges.
Boil it wll a half an Hour Skim it well all the time. Boil the rine of both in the Liquor
        1835 April 11th

Ginger Wine (2)

Put 7lb of Lisbon Sugar into 4 gallons of spring Water boil them a quarter of an hour and keep skimming it all the Time When the Liquor is could squeese in the Juice of 2 Leamons then Boul the Peal with 2 Ounces of Ginger in 3 pints of warter for an hour When it is could put it altogether into a Barrel with 2 spoonfuls of yeast a quarter of an Ounce of Issinglass beat very thin and 2lb of Raisins then Close it up let it stand 7 weeks then Bottle it off

Damson Wine

After you have gathered your damsons it must be on a dry day weigh them and then Bruise them put them into a stiens that as a cork in it and to every 8 Pounds of Fruit put a gallon of What Boil the Water skim it and pour it scalding hot on your fruit When it has stood toow days draw it of and put it into a vessel and to every gallon of Liquod put 2 and ½lb of sugar fill up the vessel and Stop it close and the longer it stands the better when you draw it off put a lump of sugar into every bottel

Grape Wine

Put a Gallon of Water to a Gallon of Grapes Bruise the Grapes well let them stand a week without stiring and draw of the Liquod put to a gallon of the wine 3lbs of Sugar and then put it into a vessel but do not fasten it down with your bung till it is don hissing let it stand 2 months and it will draw clear and fine if you think proper you may then bottle it but remember you cork it quite Close and keep it in a good Dry Celler

Ginger Beer

The Juice of 1 Leamon
½ Oz Ginger bruised
1 Ounce of Cream of Tarter
3 Ounce of moist Sugar
1 gallon of Boiling hot Water pored on the ingrediences
When Cold it is straind and put in Stone Bottles

To Make Malt Wine

To 3 Quarts of Water add one Quart of Sweetwort 3lbs of Sugar & 1lb of raisins to the gallon Boil the Liquor 20 minutes with the rine of the Leamons and Sugar skim it well Slice the Leamons & pour the hot Liquor upon them Let it 2 or 3 days put in a Barrel chop the raisins & put them in your Barrel

Apricot Wine

Put 3lb of Sugar int a Quart of Water let them Boil together and skim it well then put in six pounds of Apricots pared and stoned and let them Boil till they are tender and when the liquor is could Bottle it up for Present Use

Miscellaneous

ଔ

How to make Candy Ginger (1)

2lbs of Powder Sugur
1lb of Treacle
A bit of Butter
A little Ginger

How to make Candid Ginger (2)

2lb of Powder Sugur
½lb of Butter
A Little Ginger
Table Spoon Full of Water

Orange Jelly

6 Ounces and a half of Ising Glass disolved in ½ a pint of Water put sugar to your taste then strain and when almost cold add the Juice of one Seville Orange 6 China ones and one Leamon strain the juice of the Oranges and Leamons

How to Make Eye Water

(This recipe was written on the back cover, part of which was so worn that some words are lost)

Gather some planting leaves Boil them till quite tender. then put in a Cullander and leave to drain Rub the Liq...1 or 2 x day

Oxford Puffs

½ Egg
2 Spoonesfulls of flour
1 pint of Cream
2 Ounces of Almonds
Sugar to your taste
Leamons Peal & Brandy
nutmeg
Bake them in Earthern Cups

Orange Sponge

Dissolve 2 Ounces of Issinglass in a pint of Water and the juice of 4 Seville Oranges 1 Leamon Grate in a little juice put Sugar to your taste strain it through a sive wisk it untill it looks clear like sponge put it in a shape and Leam (?) it out this Quantity will fill a large mould & put muslin in a shape first

THE CORN MILL.

Glossary

Butter Margarine was not invented until 1869, when Napoleon III held a competition between French chemists to find a cheap substitute for butter.

Carrowe Seeds/Carrowseeds/Carroway Seeds (Caraway seeds) A biennial lacy-leaved herb of the parsley family, grown extensively in Essex in the nineteenth century.

Curriander Seeds (Coriander seeds) A feathery annual herb. In the nineteenth century coriander was grown extensively in Essex.

Custard Custard powder was invented in 1837 by Alfred Bird, who had a chemists shop in Birmingham. His wife's allergy to eggs drove him to seek an alternative to traditional custard.

Eggs: 'Free from the treadle' Treadle: 'The sperm of the cock in the egg' (Ask's *Dictionary*, 1795). The word 'treadle,' now obsolete, refers to the 'stringy' portions of the egg white which are attached to the inside of the shell. These strings were formerly thought to be sperm. The recipe requires the white to be 'free from the treadle' because cooked treadle would be lumpy and spoil the clarified sugar.

Ginger, ground, base Ginger, in the form of dried, powdered root, was one of the first oriental spices to be introduced to Europe. It was probably brought to Britain by the Romans via their African colonies. By the eighteenth century ginger had become less popular, and the fact that it features so frequently in the Georges' recipes indicates the extent to which their bakery goods were 'old fashioned.'

Hoop A large metal ring placed on a baking sheet, probably lined with brown paper. The modern equivalent is a loose-bottomed cake tin.

Isinglass/Issing Glass A highly refined and very pure form of gelatine made from the air bladder of the sturgeon or other fish. Used for the clarification of wines and beers, in jellies, or in the preservation of eggs.

Milk, Old, New As the Georges lived before the days of pasteurisation, the milk they used would have been 'straight from the cow.' The terms 'new' and 'old' referred to the amount of time the milk had been left standing.

Naples Biscuits Similar to macaroons, which can be

substituted in the recipes.

Nutmeg The inner kernel of the fruit of the nutmeg tree. The Moluccas and the islands of the Dutch East Indies were for centuries the main source of the spice. Holland, having spice markets in Amsterdam and Rotterdam, held virtually a world monopoly on the trade. Nutmeg was very popular in the seventeenth, eighteenth, and nineteenth centuries as a flavouring for sweet dishes and cakes.

Planting leaves Possibly plantain leaves?

Purlash (or Pearl-ash) A kind of baking powder. A crude potassium carbonate purified by recrystallisation. It gets its name from its pearly hue.

Rasberry Vinegar This would have been mixed with water to make a summer drink.

Sago A food starch obtained from the trunks of palms native to marshy areas of the Indonesian achipelago.

Slows (Sloes) The fruit of the hawthorn.

Steins Stein? A 'stein' was an earthernware mug which held about a pint.
    'Steen': 'A fictitious vessel of clay or stone' (Johnson's *Dictionary*, 1755).

Sugar The production of sugar from sugar cane was known from ancient times. It was not until 1744 that a German chemist established that sugar from the white beet was the same as sugar from cane. His pupil developed practical methods of extracting sugar from beet, and sugar factories spread from Prussia to France, Austria, and Russia

In 1811, Napoleon decreed the expansion of French sugar beet production. Within two years, 334 factories had opened and 35,000 tons of sugar produced. This heralded the growth of sugar production across Europe.

In the 1830s there were about a hundred sugar refineries in England and Scotland, probably refining imported cane juice. Most, if not all, of the sugar used by the George family, would therefore have been produced in Britain.

Lisbon sugar: fine white cane sugar, originally imported from Lisbon, Portugal. In the 16th century, following the explorations of Vasco da Gama, Portugal supplied the rest of Europe with sugar. By the nineteenth century Lisbon sugar was also known as 'clayed' sugar, as clay mixed with water was filtered through loaf sugar to remove the syrup. The loaves were then dried in an oven.

loaf sugar: so called from the conical loaf shape into which sugar was moulded. It was then broken up for domestic use into what was termed *lump sugar*

moist: brown sugar containing a large quantity of molasses or syrup.

powder sugar: icing sugar

sugar candy: rough pieces of whitish or yellowish sugar, sometimes on a string. The art of making sugar candy is thought to have originated in China many centuries ago, when partly clarified cane juice was boiled down to a thick mass. This was deposited, in large semi-transparent crystals on to strings or sticks which acted as nuclei.

Sugar candy was thought to be a very pure form of sugar and was probably more expensive than other types.

Sweetwort A malt wine. 'Sweet flavoured wort esp. the infusion of malt, before the hops are added in the manufacture of beer.' OED.

Treacle The residue left after sugar has been refined.

Villeta Salts, Villatic Salts, Velleta Salts
Volatile Salts, or Ammonium Carbonate, used as a raising agent. When used in baking it decomposes to carbon dioxide and water vapour, which act as the raising agents. The fact that ammonia is also given off means that it is not ideal as the smell lingers! This was also used, with the addition of perfume, as a restorative in fainting fits.

Index

Abernethy Biscuits 19
Almon (*Almond*) Cakes 17
Apple Cheese 32
Apricot Wine 38
Baked Custard Pudding 29
Best Gingerbread 18
Best Snap Gingerbread 18
Bottled Green Currants 31
Bread Pudding 29
Candy/Candid (*Candied*) Ginger (1 & 2) 39
Clarified Sugar 33
Common Gingerbread (1 & 2) 22
Common Teacakes 23
Damson Wine 37
Drop Cakes 20
Eye Water 40
Finger Biscuits 24
Gherkins (Girkins) Pickled 32
Ginger Beer 38
Gingerbread: Best Snap 18
            Best 18
            Common 22
            Thick, from Brigg 21
Ginger Cakes (1 & 2) 19
Ginger Wine (1 & 2) 36

Girkins (*Gherkins*), Pickled   32
Gooseberry Cheese   32
Grapes, Preserved Whole   31
Grape Wine   37
Maderia (*Madeira*) Buns   26
Malt Wine   38
Orange Jelly   40, Pudding   30, Sponge   41
Oxford Puffs   40
Pickled Girkins (*Gherkins*)   32
Plain and Very Crispt Biscuits   21
Plumb Cakes   24
Pound Cakes   28
Preserved Grapes, Whole   31
Queen Cakes (1 & 2)   27
Rasberry (*Raspberry*) Vinegar   35
Rice Cakes (1, 2 & 3)   25, (4)   26
Sago Pudding   30
Shape Cakes   17
Shrewsbury Biscuits   20
Slow (*Sloe*) Wine   35
Spice Cakes   24
Spunge (*Sponge*) Cakes (1 & 2)   23
Sugar, Clarified   33
Tea Cakes   20
Thick Gingerbread from Brigg   21
Wellington Cakes   21

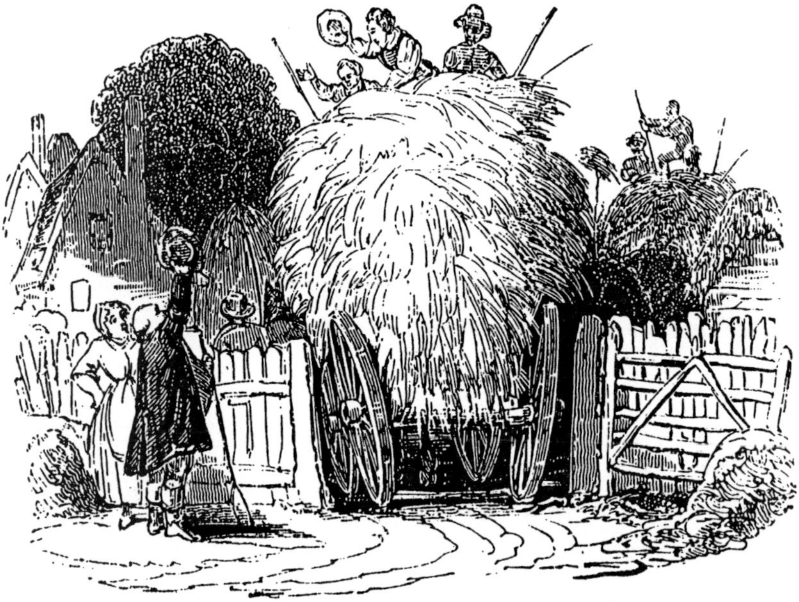